BEST OF
ATLANTIC
CANADA

FOR MY WIFE LESLIE
WHO HAS ENDURED MY EXTENSIVE TRAVELS
WITH UNFAILING SUPPORT AND LOVE.

MAGIC LIGHT PUBLISHING
OTTAWA

Newfoundland & Labrador

Nova Scotia

New Brunswick

PRINCE EDWARD ISLAND

BEST OF
ATLANTIC
CANADA

By: Jeff Hutcheson
Photography: John McQuarrie

Copyright: 2004 John McQuarrie

Published by: Magic Light Publishing
                     John McQuarrie Photography
                     192 Bruyere Street
                     Ottawa, Ontario
                     Canada   K1N 5E1

                     TEL: (613) 241-1833
                     FAX: (613) 241-2085
                     mcq@magma.ca
Bulk Sales Enquires (800) 843-0908

Design   John McQuarrie and Dave O'Malley
Printing   Paramount, Book Art, Hong Kong

Printed and bound in Hong Kong

National Library of Canada Cataloguing in Publication

Hutcheson, Jeff
        Best of Atlantic Canada / Jeff Hutcheson ; photography, John McQuarrie.

ISBN 1-894673-13-1

        1. Atlantic Provinces--Pictorial works. I. McQuarrie, John, 1946- II. Title.

FC2004.H88 2004   971.5'05'0222   C2004-900186-8

Cover: Harbour at Peggy's Cove,. John McQuarrie

Title page : Sunset, Indian Harbour. John McQuarrie

Cathedral hush of early morning fog in Chester Harbour. John McQuarrie

CONTENTS

Atlantic Canada is made up of four provinces. Each of them has tourism offices that will be happy to provide you with maps, and a wealth of information to assist with your trip planning. You will find a directory of contact information for each of these offices on the inside-back cover of this book.

But this is not a guide book – more of a highlight tour – designed to showcase many of Atlantic Canada's most popular attractions and destinations. As you journey through these pages we hope you will be inspired to visit some of our favourites and in the process, discover a few of your own.

Bon Voyage! Jeff

Photographers

Daryl Benson
Gary Black
Bill Brooks
Peter Christopher
Sherman Hines
J. A. Kraulis
Wallace MacAskill
Freeman Patterson
Greg Stott
Dale Wilson

Artists

Neil Depew
Dusan Kadlec
J. Franklin Wright

CAPE SPEAR

Aerial view of Cape Spear. John McQuarrie

Cape Spear lighthouse. John McQuarrie

North America starts here! Located just 20 minutes south of the provincial capital of St. John's, Cape Spear is the eastern most point in North America. It is an awesome feeling to stand with the Atlantic Ocean at your back and realize everyone else on the continent is west of you! And you can see the sunrise here before anyone else in North America!

This rugged, rocky shoreline is typical of the province. Step right to the edge of the cliff, with the Atlantic at your feet, and ponder the fact that you are closer to Ireland's Cape Clear, than Thunder Bay Ontario. Newfoundland and Labrador, a province so unique that it has its own time zone, did not become a part of Canada until 1949. While tourists are drawn here from all over the world, the locals come to pick partridge berries for their famous jams and jellies.

Parks Canada has turned the original lighthouse, built in 1835 into a museum. The remnants of a Second World War artillery battery, including cannons and tunnels, are here for you to explore.

Cape Spear lighthouse shrouded in typical Newfoundland fog rolling in off the Atlantic Ocean. John McQuarrie

But be prepared! This part of the country generally gets fog about 150 days of the year and if the sun is shining, count on a very brisk and bracing wind!

*The headland just visible in the distance is Signal Hill and the entrance to St. John's Harbour.
John McQuarrie*

Cape Spear. John McQuarrie

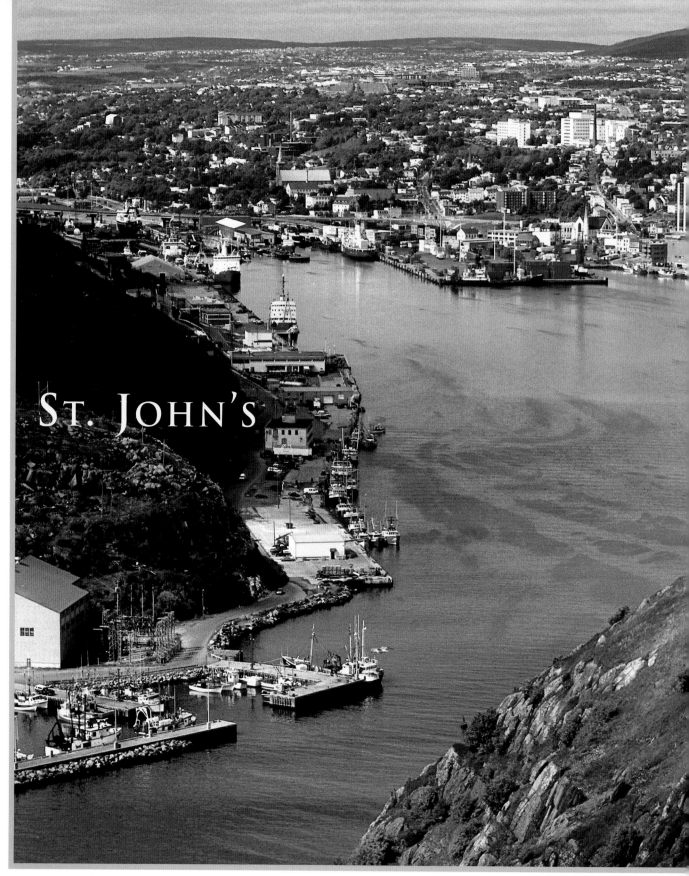

St. John's

St. John's harbour. John McQuarrie

Welcome to the oldest city in North America, St. John's, the capital of Newfoundland and Labrador. First established as a settlement over 500 years ago, the history of the city is everywhere.

The spectacular natural harbour was home to 40 vessels, 40 years before the Mayflower landed at Plymouth Rock. The Mayflower actually stopped for fresh water and food at Renews, just south of St. John's, on her maiden voyage to Plymouth Rock.

Tour boat Scademia. John McQuarrie

In 1901, at Signal Hill, with the simple word "hello", Marconi ushered in the information age by receiving the first trans Atlantic wireless transmission. But the name *Signal Hill*, has its origins in the fact that – long before Marconi – the British utilized the site for a system of flags to *signal* an approaching enemy.

I had the chance once to pilot the schooner *Scademia* (above) making its way in through the narrows. The captain asked if I knew the difference between sailing into the harbour now, as opposed to when the first European visitors did it five hundred years ago. I didn't and his answer: "No difference": It's true!

Hibernia offshore oil platform. Peter Christopher / Masterfile

A major factor in the revitalization of the economy of the province and this city of 100,000 has been the discovery of immense oil and natural gas reserves off its shores. The Hibernia oil platform on the Grand Banks in the Atlantic Ocean about 300 kilometres east of the city, sits on an estimated 600 million barrels of recoverable oil. The platform was built to withstand a collision with a one million tonne iceberg and, while that occurrence is unlikely, your chances of seeing an iceberg in the spring here are almost 100%! Just off shore from St. John's lies an ancient path known as "Iceberg Alley", where giant bergs 10,000 years in the making and freshly calved from northern glaciers, drift south.

They are just one part of what Newfoundlanders call a triple natural treat. Whales and seabirds make up the other two components of this stunning tripleheader. Over twenty species of whales, including several thousand 30 tonne humpbacks, ply these waters for food from June through August. Add to this mix millions of seabirds feeding and breeding and you've got a nature tourist's dream. The Witless Bay Ecological Reserve, home of one of the largest Puffin colonies in North America, is just down the coast from St. John's.

Summer bergs drifting through Witless Bay. Dale Wilson / Masterfile

Colourful houses typical of St. John's. Signal Hill guarding the entrance to the harbour can be seen in the background. John McQuarrie

For centuries the citizens of Newfoundland and Labrador have taken pride in their province's breathtaking beauty and unique heritage. Now the world is slowly finding out what the fuss is all about. Cruise ships carrying thousands of passengers make regular port calls in Atlantic Canada. St. John's is one of the cities enjoying the influx of visitors these liners bring in. Other cities benefiting from this tourism bonanza are Sydney and Halifax in Nova Scotia and Saint John in New Brunswick. Disembarking passengers are only a short walk away from Water Street where they can shop in the oldest store, on the oldest street, in the oldest city in North America! They can also take a short cab ride to Quidi Vidi Village which boasts its own unique harbour. Located on the eastern edge of St. John's in the shadow of Signal Hill, this picturesque little fishing village seems charmingly out of place so close to the province's capital city.

St. John's is dotted with colourful houses, a reminder of an old tradition when fishermen used to colour their homes with leftover paint from their boats. Downtown is a great place to explore with lots of history but take your walking shoes…the streets are laid out just like they were in the late 1800's, where horses and streetcars, not cars and trucks, were the mode of transportation.

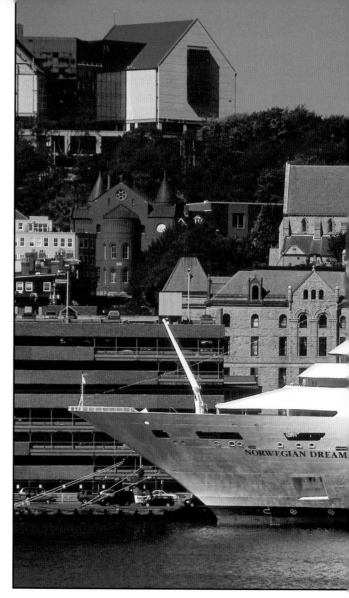

Water Street, believed to be the oldest shopping street in North America. John McQuarrie

Cruise ship docked in front of some of St. John's historic buildings.
John McQuarrie

Just minutes from downtown St. John's, the charming fishing village of
Quidi Vidi anchors the northern shore of Signal Hill. John McQuarrie

THE NARROWS

I remember the first time I laid eyes on 'the narrows', the entrance to St. John's harbour. It was dusk and a light fog hung in the air. It struck me so much that a photo of this dramatic scene hangs in my home to this day as a reminder of one of those magic moments we all experience.

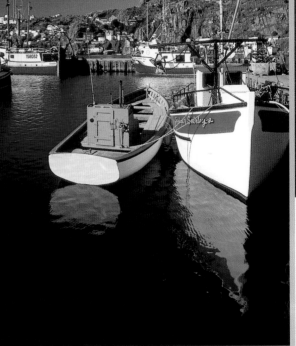

The Battery is a unique part of town where houses are literally built into the nooks and crannies of the rock cliffs that form the north face of narrows. Above the Battery – literally – is Signal Hill with its defining landmark the Cabot Tower. This would have been the last thing on land that Charles Lindbergh saw in 1927 as he embarked on his solo flight to Paris and into history. On the south side of the narrows, guarding the entrance, is Fort Amherst. It's easy to see why it was built where it was. This side of the harbour is also home to vessels of the St. John's fishing fleet

ROSE BLANCHE LIGHTHOUSE

The very granite on which it stands provided the building blocks when construction began on the Rose Blanche Lighthouse back in 1871. After two years of hard work the light was finally lit in 1873. For more than 70 years the light guarded the rugged South West Coast around Rose Blanche until it was decommissioned following the end of the Second World War.

Left unattended the historic structure quickly succumbed to the ravages of wind, water and time until it was reborn out of its own ruins in 1997. Using 70% of the original materials a small group of locals in partnership with the South West Coast Development Association breathed life back into this piece of history.

RED BAY

Right and bowhead whales, once plentiful in the waters of coastal Labrador, attracted whalers from the Basque country (northern Spain and southern France) during the 16th century. A thriving industry based on the production of whale oil for export to Europe developed along the Labrador coast during the mid to late 1500s. The busiest port for this historic enterprise was the sheltered harbour of Red Bay. Basques were expert fishermen and skilled mariners from the southeast corner of the Bay of Biscay. With the Portuguese, they were early arrivals to Newfoundland's Grand Banks.

In 16th century Europe whale oil was a precious and profitable commodity. Millions of gallons were needed for lamp fuel, lubrication, paints, varnishes and soap. Baleen, a flexible strong material found in the whale's mouth was also valued for its use in clothing and furnishings. It could be thought of as the plastic its time.

The Basques controlled the fishery along the northeast coast for more than a century. Every spring they sailed to their North America whaling stations, where they set up scaffolding to dry codfish and built stone ovens to prepare whale oil, a commodity that was highly prized in Europe. It was a profitable business but, for reasons that are unclear, the Basques whalers of France and Spain abandoned the Labrador coast around the year 1626.

Whale skull dating from the mid 16th century on the shore of Red Bay. Wandering among these bones one cannot help but be moved by the fact that they have lain in this very spot for over 400 years. Saddle Island can be seen to the right and the village of Red Bay is visible at top left

It has long been known that during the 16th century, fishermen from Europe were seasonally fishing off the coast of Canada. It was not until the 1970s however, that documentary research uncovered evidence of numerous Basque whaling ports along the coast of Labrador. At Red Bay, extensive archaeological remains have been discovered. Visitors to the Red Bay National Historic Site can view a wealth of artifacts and exhibits explaining this fascinating part of the history of the Labrador coast.

Boardwalk and interpretive panels along the shore of Saddle Island, Red Bay. John McQuarrie

Visitor Interpretation Centre and Boat Landing, Red Bay. John McQuarrie

John McQuarrie

Shipwreck off Saddle Island, Red Bay. Interestingly, this ship foundered in a storm in 1965, exactly 400 years after the same fate befell the San Juan, a ship laden with close to a thousand barrels of whale oil, which broke its anchor and sank less than 100 yards from the site of this rusty wreck. John McQuarrie

BATTLE HARBOUR

Once the luxurious residence of the fishing merchants, this beautiful house is now the Battle Harbour Inn. *John McQuarrie*

Battle Harbour General Store is a prime example of the old-fashioned shop common to coastal communities in days gone by.

John McQuarrie

View of Battle Harbour from Great Caribou Island. John McQuarrie

Once the site of a thriving salt fish, salmon and seal processing complex, Battle Harbour was the economic and social centre of the entire coast, known to one and all as the unofficial capital of Labrador. The salt fish plantation at Battle Harbour was established by the firm of John Slade and Company of Poole, England in the 1770s. The Slade premises became the major base for the region's fisheries. The site was operated by several companies until it was abandoned with the collapse of the cod fishery in the early 1990s.

Eclipsed in recent decades by changing economies and settlement patterns, the former glory of Battle Harbour has now been revived. Six years of research and painstaking architectural restoration have breathed new life into this unique, historic place.

Through the efforts of the Battle Harbour Historic Trust, the village of Battle Harbour is now a living commemoration of the life and society created there by Newfoundlanders and Labradoreans during the 18th, 19th and 20th centuries.

L 'Anse Aux Meadows

In the past four to five thousand years, many people have lived at l'Anse aux Meadows; some stayed longer than others. Among these people was a small group of Norse sailors. The remains of their camp, discovered in 1960 by Helge and Anne Stine Ingstad, is the oldest known European settlement of the New World.

Reconstructed Viking settlement. John McQuarrie

L'Anse aux Meadows, the centrepiece of what Newfoundlanders refer to as Viking country, is located at the top of the great Northern Peninsula. The area is remote and your journey to this national historic site will take you through such places as Anchor Point, Deadman's Cove, Nameless Cove and Eddie's Cove. The payoff to your time and travel is fantastic. L'Anse aux Meadows is the place where the Vikings established the first European settlement in North America over 1000 years ago. Native people had occupied this land for thousands of years before the newcomers arrived. According to Norse legend, sailor Bjarni Herjolfsson was blown off course sailing from Iceland to Greenland in 986. When he finally made port in Greenland, he reported seeing three new 'lands', believed to be north and south Labrador and Newfoundland.

He and his crew were the first Europeans to see North America. About 15 years later, Norse explorer Leif Erickson finally set foot on this 'new land' that Herjolfsson had discovered. He and his 30-man crew set up a small community around the year 1000. No one knows for sure how long they stayed. After they left the earthen buildings of the small community decayed and nature reclaimed the land for a long, long time. In 1960, the remains of this camp were discovered; and now, the reconstructions of three Norse buildings form the focal point of this UNESCO World Heritage Site. These sod houses give visitors a taste of what life must have been like for those hearty souls. As early as the 1920s, Newfoundland author W.A. Munn had suggested that the 'Vinland' referred to in Norse Sagas might well be L'Anse aux Meadows and he could well be right!

Visitor Centre. John McQuarrie

NORSTEADT

Located just two kilometres from L'Anse aux Meadows, Norsteadt represents how a Viking settlement might have evolved had they stayed longer in their new world.

Church and blacksmith shop. John McQuarrie

Interpreters dressed in period clothing take on the roll of various members of Viking society and give visitors information in the first person. For people willing to imagine themselves transported back over a thousand years, this unique way of explaining the various features of the settlement and how life would have been lived here so long ago, adds another dimension to any visit.

Interior of chieftans hall, gathering place where everyone took their meals. John McQuarrie.

John Cabot Sighting Cape Bonavista. Harold Goodridge,
in 1947 for the 450th anniversary of Cabot's voyage of discovery

Locally built Matthew replica docked at the Matthew Legacy site in Bonavista Harbour. John McQuarrie

Here is the story of the discovery of the New Founde Landes...

Imagine the wind whistling through the sails, seagulls soaring overhead and the gentle rolling of a 15th century Caravel. As you look out to sea you dream of what it must have felt like for John Cabot in 1497 as he sailed across the uncharted Atlantic.

When Columbus returned from the Americas in 1493 it is highly likely that *Giovanni Caboto* – or John Cabot as he came to be known today – would have set out to meet him, given that both had once lived in Genoa.

Matthew Legacy site, Bonavista Harbour. John McQuarrie

Five years after Columbus discovered land in the Caribbean, Cabot set sail for the new world from Bristol, England on May 2nd, 1497. After failing to convince the kings of Spain and Portugal that there had to be a westward trading route to the silks and spices of Asia, he turned to King Henry VII. The English monarch was so impressed by the young man that he arranged for financial backing by several wealthy merchants. Cabot soon set sail on the *Matthew*, named for his wife Mattea, and a relatively short 34 days later, he set foot in Newfoundland.

Before setting course for home, Cabot sailed 900 miles down the North American coast and discovered the Grand Banks. This vast cod habitat was so rich that it helped to stimulate English colonization of the continent.

A year later, Cabot and five ships set sail on another voyage of discovery, but they were never heard from again. His initial voyage though, did mark the beginning of migration that has come to characterize the very nature of North America

Today, Bonavista is one of Newfoundland and Labrador's most famous towns. Locals will tell you that getting 'lost', which apparently is easy to do, is the best way to see the town. Make sure you see the Mockbegger Plantation Provincial Historic Site and the Ryan Premises National Historic Site. These properties will give you a taste of life in nineteenth century Newfoundland along with a 500-year history of the east coast fishery.

At Sweetland's Bank you'll find a replica of the *Mathew*, John Cabot's ship. To commemorate the 500-year anniversary of the voyage to the new world the province commissioned the construction of the ship that is another 'don't miss' destination. Incidentally, Cabot Tower on Signal Hill in St. John's was built in 1897 to commemorate the 400th anniversary of Cabot's arrival on the shores of Newfoundland.

Bonavista Memorial United Church. John McQuarrie

PLACENTIA

Steeped in history, Placentia is located on the Cape Shore in the western portion of the Avalon region. Basque fishermen had been coming here as early as the 16th century, attracted by the large quantities of codfish, highly prized in Europe.

The French founded the settlement in 1662, naming it *Plaisance* and making it the French capital of Newfoundland. The present day Castle Hill National Historic Site was the 1692 location of the French fortification called *Le Gaillardin*. From this position the French attacked English forces in St. John's three times. While they were repelled each time they did manage to burn down the city on one of their forays.

Today, the remains of France's 17th-century fortress at Castle Hill are all that is left of the French presence here. Events in Europe sealed Plaisance's fate when the British gained sovereignty over Newfoundland by the Treaty of Utrecht, leaving France with fishing rights restricted to the northeast and west coasts. Visitors to this national historic site can walk among the ruins of Le Gaillardin, learning a little about the people and events that shaped this part of Atlantic Canada.

Placentia Bay also played a key role during the Second World War. The eastern Atlantic was considered vulnerable to German attack and the Allies rushed construction of new defence bases. Work at nearby Argentia began in 1940 and the base was ready by mid 1941. By 1943, 7500 men were stationed at the base.

Ship Harbour, in Placentia Bay was the scene of one of the War's most important meetings. In August of 1941, US President Franklin D. Roosevelt and British Prime Minister Winston Churchill held secret talks to discuss their visions for a prosperous post-war world. From these meetings came the "Atlantic Charter", which subsequently became the basis for the founding declaration of the United Nations.

British warships under Commodore Williams attacking Ft. Louis, 1692. © Dusan Kadlec
(Opposite) Fishing fleet in Placentia Harbour. John McQuarrie
(Below) Dramatic view of Placentia from the fortifications on Castle Hill National Historic Site. John McQuarrie

CAPE ST. MARY'S

(Previous page and above)
The Northern Gannet colony at St. Mary's numbers some 5400 nesting pairs, most of which make their home on spectacular Bird Rock.   John McQuarrie

Atlantic Puffins, Witless Bay Seabird Ecological Reserve, Bauline East.
Photos courtesy of Ocean Adventure, Bauline East. (Oceanadventure.ca)

At the southwest tip of the Avalon Peninsula, washed on three sides by the restless Atlantic, lies Cape St. Mary's – one of the most spectacular (and most accessible!) seabird colonies in North America. This park, one of six seabird ecology reserves protected by the Newfoundland and Labrador Provincial Park System, protects hundreds of thousands of birds who breed and nest on the islands and coastal cliffs of this rugged landscape. For over a century, naturalists and lovers of the outdoors have been drawn here, amazed by the immensity, the whirling clamour of 60,000 seabirds and the awesome power of giant whales.

Bird Rock and the adjacent cliffs are like avian high-rise apartment towers. The ledges, outcrops, overhangs and plateaus offer a variety of accommodation for a variety of seabird species. Each has found a niche that suits its particular nesting requirements. This formation, a sea stack standing directly adjacent to the main body of the headland just offshore, rises 100 metres from the sea. Millions of years of erosion have worn away the softer limestone that once connected the rock pinnacle to the cliff, creating a natural refuge from the land-based predators of seabird eggs and chicks and making Bird Rock the second largest gannetry in North America.

Comprised of four small islands and the water around them, the Witless Bay Ecological Reserve is one of the greatest natural wonders in the world. In summer it is home to millions of seabirds that come to shore to nest and raise their young. They include birds like Murres, Great Black-Backed Gulls and Black Legged Kittiwakes. Thousands of humpback whales feed here in summer, making it one of the best whale-watching areas anywhere.

Here is the largest Atlantic Puffin colony in North America. Known affectionately as 'Sea Parrots', the charming Puffin is also the Provincial Bird of Newfoundland and Labrador. Puffins are true seabirds and as such spend most of their time at sea, swimming, diving, and feeding. For about 4– 5 months every year they come to land to breed, but even then they spend a lot of time at sea. Puffins return to colonies in Newfoundland around mid-April. Puffins normally keep the same mate and the same burrow from year to year. The average bird lives about 20 years.

TRINITY

Drive north from Clarenville on Route 230, taking a right onto Route 239 - Trinity Harbour comes into view like unwrapping a present.   John McQuarrie

This small village is considered a national treasure and most of the old town is a national heritage community. Those interested in Newfoundland history will find it in Trinity. According to local folklore, the village got its name because it was discovered on Trinity Sunday in 1501, just four years after John Cabot set foot in nearby Bonavista. The English considered the town site so valuable and the harbour so important that it became one of the few communities in Newfoundland to have the Crown build a fort for protection.

The remains of the fort are accessible via a gravel road to the lighthouse. If you're visiting on a summer day this spot offers a wonderful place to whale watch!

Trinity is a village of narrow lanes and well-constructed 19th century houses. Much has been preserved in this once prosperous and progressive town. In the late 1700's, it made history when a local doctor administered the first smallpox vaccine in North America.

View of part of the town including St. Paul's Anglican Church and the town's lighthouse on Fort Point in the distance. John McQuarrie
(Below) Cannons at Fort Point mark the location of the English fort that once guarded the harbour. John McQuarrie

What strikes you right away about Trinity is how solid the houses are. The nineteenth century styles of architecture that are preserved seem derived from an earlier era. Get out and wander around Trinity's narrow lanes.

By the way, there is another Trinity in the Bonavista Bay area. It's on route 320. The little gem we're talking about here, is on route 239 - just so you know!

The Lester-Garland Premises, St. Paul's Anglican Church and Parish Hall. John McQuarrie

View of Trinity Bay and Fort Point Light from town. John McQuarrie

TRINITY BIGHT

View of entrance to Old Bonaventure Harbour and Trinity Bay. John McQuarrie

Old Bonaventure Cemetary. John McQuarrie

At first glance, epitaphs might seem a little out of place in a book focussing on travel. But they often tell intriguing stories that can offer a sense of how lives were lived in a particular place. And nowhere is this more so than in Newfoundland. Look at these two examples. Here is a powerful statement showing the sheer randomness of life. How did it work out that Joseph Clarke enjoyed 72 good years in this place while the three King children 'departed' way before their time? They also point to the obvious fact that life was tough in this part of the world in the 19th century. What calamity killed these three kids? Perhaps a house fire - or was it disease? Imagine the pain of the parents as their three children were torn from them in as many weeks. Then turn around and imagine these young people playing on these same streets so many years ago. The place probably didn't look all that different in 1863 than it did on the day I took these photos.   John McQuarrie

Cape Random, a village built for the filming of the international TV mini-series "Random Passage", offers visitors the opportunity to imagine life in a fishing community in the early 1800's. The top photo shows a fish stage on the set but the cod you see drying in the sun are plastic. John McQuarrie

A *bight* is the bend in a coast forming an open bay. Trinity Bight, from the north shore, contains the communities of English Harbour, Champney's East, Champney's Arm, Champney's West, Trinity East, Port Rexton, Trinity, Goose Cove, Dunfield, Trouty, Old Bonaventure and New Bonaventure. These communities are gems - colonial culture brightened by buoyant palettes of Atlantic colours: the sea, sky, hills and the carefully applied paint on treasured homes and buildings.

Brilliant summer comes alive in the historically significant communities of Trinity Bight. The deep regard and respect for the past goes back farther here than anywhere else on the island.

The lovely wooden church, St. Luke's, which was established in 1892 can be seen overlooking fishing boats in Old Bonaventure Harbour at right.

Petty Harbour. John McQuarrie

Old Bonaventure. John McQuarrie

OUTPORTS

Newfoundland is dotted with little fishing villages known as outports. For years, many could only be reached by boat and these villages spawned a cohesive local society born of isolation and united by their fishing dependent economies. These various societies preserved their folk characteristics of custom, language and music.

Diamond Cove. John McQuarrie

Rose Blanche. John McQuarrie

It is said there are almost 100 different dialects in the province, and the isolation of these outports is the root cause. To this day these villages, many of them now abandoned, stand as a poignant reminder of the resilience of an independent people shaped by a harsh climatic, economic and political environment.

Outports also had local meeting places for food and drink. Those establishments featured elements drawn from the British pub, the waterfront seaman's tavern and the newly re-discovered Newfoundland gastronomy. Items like cod tongue and cheeks, seal flipper pie, moose stew and cod 'n brewis were local favourites. These delicacies have now found their way into eating establishments, new and old, right across the province.

Rocky Harbour. John McQuarrie

S.S. Kyle has been a fixture of Riverhead, Harbour Grace since being abandoned here in 1967 after sustaining extensive ice damage. She began service on the ferry route between Port aux Basques and North Sydney in 1913 and subsequently on the Newfoundland–Labrador run. Towards the end of her distinguished career she enjoyed the distinction of being one of the last steam-powered vessels to be used in commercial service. John McQuarrie

Picturesque Brigus on Conception Bay was an active fishing and sealing centre throughout the 19th century. It was also home to Captain Bob Bartlett the master mariner and arctic explorer. John McQuarrie

Hawthorne Cottage National Historic Site in Brigus offers a glimpse into the colourful life of Captain Robert Bartlett. In 1908, Bartlett was captain of the Roosevelt, the ship that took Robert E. Peary to Ellesmere Island, prior to his trip to the North Pole. John McQuarrie

Harbour Grace Court House is one of the oldest institutional buildings in the province having been in continuous use as a Court House from the time of its construction in 1830. Only in recent years has the use of the prisoner's cells in the jail portion been discontinued. John McQuarrie

Harbour Grace on Conception Bay is a leading fishing port and fish-processing centre. Settled c.1550, it is also one of the oldest towns in the province. John McQuarrie

LOBSTER COVE HEAD

Constructed in 1887, this lighthouse at Rocky
Harbour in Gros Morne National Park is now a
museum. The site offers visitors stunning views of
the Gulf of St. Lawrence both from atop the cliff
and – via a series of easy trails – the beautiful little cove from which this photograph was taken.

John McQuarrie

Aerial view of downtown Halifax with the Historic Properties–Privateers Wharf spread out before you along the waterfront. John McQuarrie

HALIFAX

It's not hard to see why this settlement became an important naval base dating as far back as the mid-1700's. Halifax harbour, which extends 26 kilometres inland from the Atlantic Ocean, offered unlimited natural protection to the Royal Navy and in later years, the Royal Canadian Navy. While Canada's eastern Navy still calls the city home, today's Halifax features a wonderful marriage of the recently restored Historic Properties-Privateer's Wharf area along the harbour and the more contemporary architecture that overlooks it all.

A centrepiece of the harbour, the Maritime Museum of the Atlantic commemorates the city's vital link with the sea and seafaring life through its displays of over 20,000 maritime artifacts. On my first visit to the museum I made a beeline up the stairs straight to the Titanic exhibit. It's here you'll find an original deck chair from the ill-fated ocean liner and the story of the Halifax connection to the disaster. Close by you'll find artifacts from the devastating Halifax explosion of 1917 when the Belgium relief ship *Imo* collided with the French munitions ship the *Mont Blanc*.

Preparing for the lunch crowd at harbourside. John McQuarrie

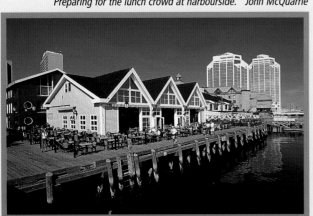

A Halifax landmark, Salty's anchors the eastern flank of Halifax's Historic Properties–Privateers Wharf on the harbour. John McQuarrie

The star-shaped Citadel occupies the high ground .   John McQuarrie

View to the north up George Street toward the landmark Clock Tower.

The *CSS Acadia*, Canada's first Hydrographic vessel and *HMCS Sackville*, the last of the World War II convoy escort Corvettes draw thousands of visitors every year. Canada's Naval Memorial, *Sackville* is maintained and operated by the Canadian Naval Memorial Trust, a non-profit society.

Great cities the world over often owe their location to early military considerations. While admirals looked to safe harbours, generals sought out hilltops. Halifax offered both.

Located on a hill overlooking downtown Halifax, the star shaped Citadel took 28 years to complete. Its purpose was to protect the city from a land based attack that never came and it remains in pristine condition to this day as a national historic site. The massive green space around the fort that would once have discouraged any invader is enjoyed today as a scene for more peaceful pursuits from picnics to outdoor concerts.

Halifax is fortunate that it has any history at all. In 1917, The French munitions ship *Mont Blanc* collided with the steamer Imo, and the resulting explosion leveled the north end of the city, leaving 2,000 dead and many thousands more homeless. But somehow most of the historic buildings survived. One of the great beauties of the city is the compactness of its downtown. A stroll along the living history of the harbourside boardwalk and up to the Citadel, requires a walk of just a few blocks.

Dartmouth ferry enroute to Halifax.   John McQuarrie

The Halifax Citadel is one of Canada's most visited national historic sites.   John McQuarrie

Pier 21 continues to welcome visitors to Halifax but today it is tourists rather than immigrants who disembark from luxurious cruise ships. John McQuarrie
www.pier21.ns.ca

Pier 21, the newest addition to the attractions on the waterfront, was the first place that one million immigrants experienced upon arrrival in Canada between 1928 and 1971.

Beautifully renovated, it is now a national historic site celebrating Canada's rich immigrant heritage through a series of imaginative exhibits.

A glorious summer afternoon on the harbourfront.
John McQuarrie

Province House, seat of the provincial government. John McQuarrie
Writer Charles Dickens called Province House "a gem of Georgian architecture" and described the 1842 opening of the legislature as being "like looking at Westminster through the wrong end of the telescope".

Rising sun creates a lovely glow within the fog blanketing West Dover harbour. John McQuarrie

Morning fog adds a special quiet beauty to this small lake nestled between Peggy's Cove and West Dover. The boulders you see in these photos are typical of the area. They are actually 415 million year old "Devonian" granite deposited here by the last retreating glaciers about 10,000 years ago. It is interesting to think that the boulders you see silhouetted on the ridge line in this photo – however precarious their perch may appear – have not moved since the last ice age.

On the barrens you will find blueberries, cranberries, black berries and huckelberries. These rocks are also home to the Pitcher plant, a carnivorous flower that lures insects into the small pool of water within its flowering bulb. The unsuspecting fly is then trapped by the plant and consumed. Lupines and wild Iris also abound, but please do not pick these plants. They are here for all to enjoy.

PEGGY'S COVE

Perhaps the most famous lighthouse in all of Canada is situated at Peggy's Cove on Nova Scotia's picturesque south shore. near Halifax. Perched on an outcropping of rocks over 400 million years old, this famous beacon is no longer operational in its warning and lifesaving role for mariners. But come the high tourist season in the summer months, it is used as a post office, complete with its own cancellation stamp. Naturally, the stamp is... a lighthouse!

The tiny fishing village of Peggy's Cove is part of the much larger and equally scenic St. Margaret's Bay, and likely got its name because "Peggy" is a common nickname for Margaret. But, there is also folklore to be considered. The more romantic version has the village named after the sole survivor of a 19th century shipwreck, washed up on the rocks during a hurricane. Legend has it that the young "Peggy" married one of her rescuers – a local fisherman – and lived happily ever after!

The harbour is so small you are seeing almost all of it in the picture at top right. Tucked in behind the lighthouse this little cove evolved naturally as a place of safe harbour.

For obvious reasons, the area is a summer Mecca for artists and photographers. Its stunning sunsets and friendly local flavour only add to the many reasons to visit. The very name Peggy's Cove is synonymous with the natural, unspoiled beauty of Nova Scotia's south shore.

Three views of Peggy's Cove. John McQuarrie

Morning fog puts another face of Peggy's Cove Lighthouse. John McQuarrie

Peggy's Cove Lighthouse reflecting the first light of a summer morning and (inset) a seagull's eye view. *John McQuarrie*

There are several places in Canada where I consider the actual visit to be an *experience*. One of these is Peggy's Cove. If you've never been there it's everything you've ever imagined and more, yet all so simple. A lighthouse, perched on 400 million year old granite guards the entrance to St. Margaret's Bay.

That's it. Nature does the rest. The power of nature is brought home by a warning sign, one that you encounter as you venture out onto the rocks. It warns of the danger of high waves crashing onto the rocks and the fate that awaits if you get too close. This is not the place you want to go for a swim. It's all part of the *experience*.

I vividly recall one sunny June day here. Two sailboats glided by just as if someone had ordered them up to add to my *experience*. A few moments later my attention was drawn to people scurring to the edge of the rocks to watch whales frolicking no more than 200 metres off shore. It's that *experience* thing again. Peggy's Cove is one of my favourite places to be in all of Canada.

Peggy's Cove bathed in first light of a summer morning and a winter afternoon. John McQuarrie

HARBOUR MIST

The image and aura surrounding Peggy's Cove was forever changed on that terrible night of September 2nd, 1998 when, just a few kilometres off shore, Swissair Flight 111 was lost. Fishermen from the cove were among the first to join the search for survivors. In the years since the accident, families of the victims and residents of Peggy's Cove have developed strong personal bonds and friendships. Many residents continue to open their homes to families who visit the area each September to remember lost family members and spend time at the shoreline in quiet reflection.

Enscription on the memorial to Swissair Flight 111:

**In memory of
the 229 men, women and children
aboard Swissair Flight 111
who perished off these shores
September 2nd, 1998,
They have been joined to the sea, and the sky.
May they rest in peace.**

In the midst of taking photographs of this lovely sunset, with charming fiddle music providing an almost unbearably perfect accompaniment to this magic moment, I became aware of a young woman talking quietly on her cell phone. Initially my reaction was negative. How could anyone talk on the phone at such a moment? But when her soft-spoken words reached me, my feelings quickly changed. She was sitting on a rock, off by herself, talking to her mother. And - that's right - she was describing how moved she was by the beauty of the moment as that sun slipped gently behind the far shore of St. Margaret's Bay.

Someone once wrote "There is no joy in anything unshared." Part of the human condition is the need to share the experiences and events of our lives that touch us and, being alone, this was how she chose to respond to that need. I suppose this explains why most travel packages are based on double occupancy.

John McQuarrie

Busking sisters provide a charming accompaniment to the setting sun on a lovely summer evening at Peggy's Cove. John McQuarrie

BLUENOSE II

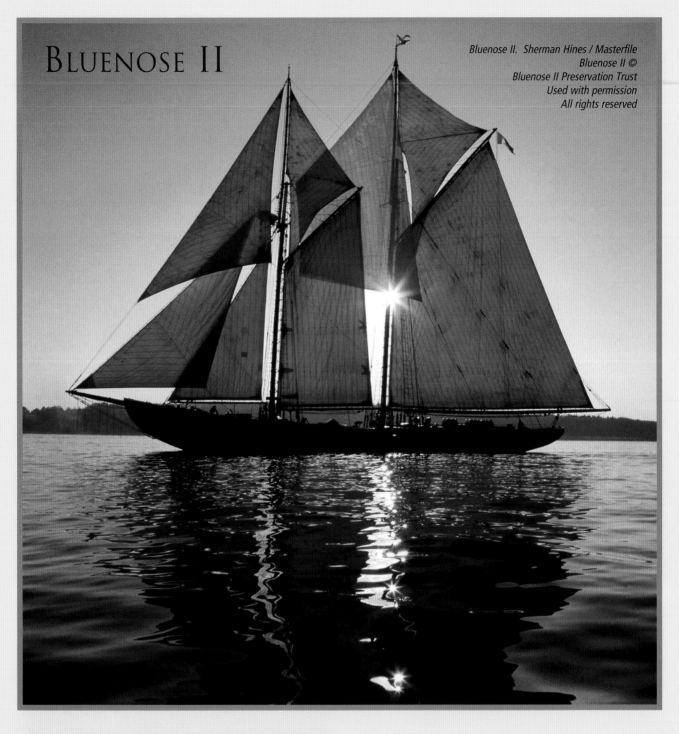

Since 1937, the schooner *Bluenose* has graced the back of the Canadian dime. The original *Bluenose* was a fishing vessel that doubled as the world's fastest ship on the water. She took on American challengers in the International Fishermen's Trophy races, and from 1921 to the final race in 1938, she was never beaten. Eventually sold to carry freight in the Caribbean, the *Bluenose* was lost on a Haitian reef in January of 1946. But rebirth occurred in a shipyard in Lunenburg early in the 1960's. Using the identical plans, and some of the same shipbuilders that worked on the original *Bluenose*, *Bluenose II* picked up the torch when she was launched in July of 1963. Owned by the province, *Bluenose II* spends her summers in the waters off Atlantic Canada, ready to take you on the sail of a lifetime!

International Fisherman's Trophy Race, First Elimination Contest 1921.
Alcala follows on heels of Independence while Canadia and Bluenose
can be seen out in front.   Wallace MacAskill, 1987-453/ 206

Deck detail during storm off Grand Bank fishing schooner Bluenose
(from Starboard Lookout series)
Wallace MacAskill, Nova Scotia Archives, 1987-453/ 226

A Nova Scotian born and bred, Wallace MacAskill ([1887] - 1956) was one of the first Canadian photographers to achieve distinction in international salons where his work was not only admired for its technical excellence but for the truth of its statements about men and the sea. One of MacAskill's photographs of the *Bluenose* became the subject of a commemorative postage stamp issued in 1929 and in 1937 and another appeared on the Canadian ten cent coin.

MacAskill's wonderful photographs and the magnificent paintings by maritime artists like Dusan Kadlec provide a lasting legacy to this Canadian icon and the golden age of sail.

Bluenose and Henry Ford, Fisherman's Trophy race, 1926. Courtesy Dusan Kadlec ©

Spirit of Massachusetts and Bluenose II off Lunenburg. John McQuarrie

Spirit of Massachusetts is modeled after the fishing schooner *Fredonia*, designed by Edward Burgess in 1889. Like *Bluenose*, these schooners were famous throughout the world as the "fast and able" vessels of the North Atlantic fisheries, sailing winter and summer to the rich grounds of the Grand Banks and Georges Bank. *Spirit* was built in the Charlestown Navy Yard in Boston in 1984 for service as a sail training ship operated by the Ocean Classroom Foundation. (www.sailgamage.org)

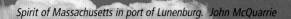

Spirit of Massachusetts in port of Lunenburg. John McQuarrie

Bluenose II departing Lunenburg. John McQuarrie

If there's anything more beautiful than a wooden schooner in the picture-postcard setting of Lunenburg, it could only be *two* of these magnificent vessels. During the weekend of The Lunenburg Fishermen's Picnic & Reunion in August of 2003, *Spirit of Massachusetts* arrived in port escorted by that town's pride and joy, *Bluenose II*.

Bluenose II under sail. John McQuarrie   Bluenose II © , Bluenose II Preservation Trust., Used with permission. All rights reserved

Lunenburg harbour. John McQuarrie

LUNENBURG

One of Nova Scotia's most picturesque and historic towns is Lunenburg on the province's south shore. History drips from the town of 2,600 which was designated a UNESCO World Heritage Site in 1995 to recognize it as an outstanding example of a planned European colonial settlement. The area was first settled by French, German and Swiss immigrants in 1753, and some of the oldest churches in the country, built by those settlers, still stand.

Lunenburg is one of the best fishing ports in North America but, despite all its history, the town's chief claim to fame remains the honour of being the birthplace of Canada's legendary racing schooner, Bluenose, and her replica, Bluenose II.

The Fisheries Museum of the Atlantic, complete with five waterfront buildings and two historic ships, stands as a testament to maritime life in Atlantic Canada. Lunenburg is one of many jewels along the province's Lighthouse Route which unfailingly hugs the breathtaking south shore of Nova Scotia.

Fishing boats and docks just north of Lunenburg. John McQuarrie

MAGIC LOBSTER

This is not really a recipe. More like a Canadian ritual. And if you follow it precisely the experience will remain with you longer than most.

Preparation Time: Your life 'till this moment
Cooking Time: 0

Ingredients:
2 market lobsters, cooked
1 bottle Nova Scotia white wine
1 medium sized rock (about 2 lbs)
1 corkscrew
No butter
No garlic
No salt or pepper

Ideally you will be on a journey through the Maritimes when a roadside sign beckons: "Cooked Lobsters". Packed in ice – along with your wine – they will travel nicely for several hours as you search out your private dining place by the sea. Take the first side road where the sign includes the word "wharf". Best time is early evening, your pier quiet, atmosphere just right. Set yourself down on the edge of the dock, lobsters, rock and wine at hand. Gently tap the claws with said rock until they crack and *voila*, your meal is served. Tail and body can be opened with your hands so no utensils are required. As you savour your simple meal from the sea, by the sea, toss the scraps into the ocean where they will not go unappreciated.

Then let your mind wander, enjoying the lovely places it takes you.

John McQuarrie

FISHERIES MUSEUM OF THE ATLANTIC

No trip to Lunenburg is complete without a visit to the world-class Fisheries Museum of the Atlantic. It commemorates the fishing heritage of the Atlantic Coast of Canada and you can't miss its brightly painted red buildings and floating museum vessels at wharf side.

Nova Scotia's famous schooner *Bluenose* is celebrated here in an exhibit that features the world's largest collection of *Bluenose* artifacts, including the famous International Fisherman's Trophy. On the second floor you'll find Lunenburg's Fisherman's Memorial Room, a tribute to those lost at sea.

You'll also learn about the "August gales" of 1926 and 1927. To this day it's hard to find anyone in the Lunenburg/Blue Rocks area that didn't lose a relative in those fierce "perfect" storms that sank a total of six ships in August of 1926, and unbelievably, again in August of 1927. The ships were based in Lunenburg and fishing off Sable Island. Over 130 souls were lost at sea in the ravages of these storms. In many cases men from entire families were wiped out. The 1927 sinking of the *Mahala* claimed 8 members of Lunenburg's Knickle family. It's a Canadian disaster few outside the area know about.

The Old Fish Factory Restaurant is attached to the museum and features, of course, all the seafood you can eat along with plenty of that great Nova Scotian hospitality. Incidently, a favourite toast for Nova Scotians is " Sociable!"

Fog caresses floating exhibits of the Fisheries Museum of the Atlantic, Lunenburg. John McQuarrie

Fisheries Museum of the Atlantic, Lunenburg. John McQuarrie

On the Banks
Image courtesy of
J. Franklin Wright.
www.downtoearth.com

American and Canadian dory racing teams preparing for the final half mile course for the championship. John McQuarrie

Oar shafts bend as the dorymen dig in for the championship run. John McQuarrie

By the 1920's, the indomitable fishing schooner had reached the apex of its development. Fore-and-aft rigged, the typical two-masted "Grand Banker" was primarily engaged in the salt-cod fishery. A fast and weatherly "saltbanker" such as *Bluenose*, would go out to the rich fishing grounds of the Grand Banks for cod. The fish were split and salted in bulk down in the hold until the schooner was full.

Usually built with a bottom length of 12 - 16 feet, a dory could carry two men equipped with bait and fishing gear for handlining or trawl fishing and up to 2,000 lbs of cod. John McQuarrie

The rugged dory fishermen of this period were the most respected men on the North Atlantic. Day after day, year after year, in oppressive fog, blinding snow squalls, and savage storms, they toiled for hours at a time, on frigid and unforgiving seas.

The "Banks Dory", as it became known, was ideally suited for use aboard fishing schooners. It was lightweight but strongly built, an important feature since the dory had to be hoisted and lowered from the schooner, often with the equipment and day's catch still in the dory. Once aboard the schooner, the removable thwarts, or seats, allowed it to be nested on top of other dories to save space on deck, an important feature when a schooner's complement of dories could number as many as 14. In the water, the flat-bottomed dory was difficult to handle when not loaded, however laden with fishing gear, it became more stable and rowed or sailed very easily.

Today this rich heritage is kept alive by dory building shops - most notably, those in Shelburne and Lunenburg. The dory builders skills are given life every summer during the famous dory races that highlight the annual Lunenburg Fishermen's Picnic & Reunion held every August.

I had the chance to participate in one of these dory races and believe me; you get a whole new appreciation for the men who manned these vessels. I was involved in a five dory race once, set up to give me a taste of this famous annual event. The distance was one half mile on a course set up in the harbour. I had never been so exhausted, tired, aching and sore...and we were only at the half way marker! Jeff

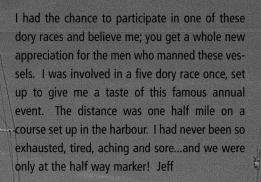

Warm summer nights can be relied upon to whip up an enchanting fog that will slowly release its grip on the coast as the ever-warming air absorbs the microscopic water droplets temporarily suspended in the atmosphere. In the large image above fishing boats in the harbour at Blue Rocks are barely visible from shore but, just an hour later the sun has transformed the scene completely – as evidenced in the photograph at right, taken from the same spot. Later in the day the tide has risen and a group of kayakers are coming in for their shore lunch. John McQuarrie

CHESTER

Chester and Mahone Bay, two charming villages along Nova Scotia's south shore Lighthouse Route, offer visitors the chance to experience the seaside life of another era. It's a drive worth taking and taking all the way down the coast. Chester is the type of place you think you will see only in the movies. Summertime is special here. The village of just over 1200 is noted for its regal homes, quiet tree lined streets, fabulous views and quaint atmosphere. If you perch yourself on the main waterfront near the yacht club, you'll have a great view of some of the picturesque offshore islands that are seemingly just a stones-throw away and look a bit out of place! The 'well-heeled' are in Chester to be sure. Spectacular summer homes and luxurious yachts are everywhere. The yachting crowd mingles seamlessly with local fishermen. Your view of the Chester Basin from the circular parking area near the cenotaph is worth the trip alone. Since 1827 when Chester's first hotel was built, people have been drawn to its elegant seaside charm. Now locals no doubt cringe every time they read about their town in a book like this. I'd want to keep it a secret too!

Chester Harbour is a Mecca for well-to-do sailors and yachtsmen who have built luxurious vacation homes throughout the Chester Basin. An abundance of classic yachts fill the harbour during the summer season. Shrouded in the morning mist, one could easily imagine having been transported back in time to the 1920's of the Great Gatsby. John McQuarrie

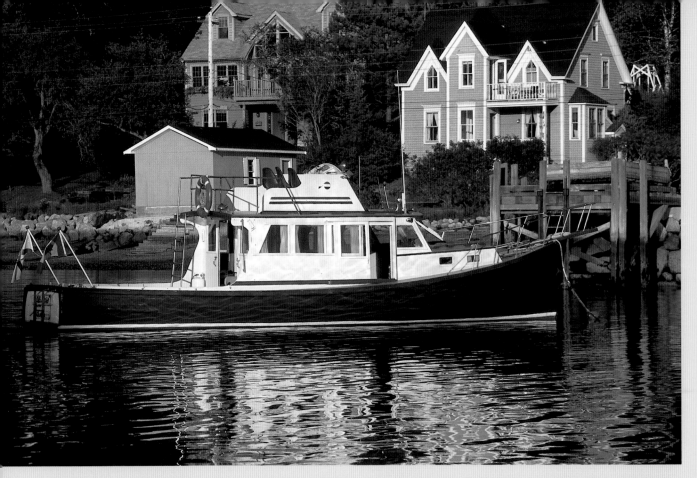

Chester is also a jumping-off point for an adventure to one of Nova Scotia's hidden treasures, the Tancook Islands at the mouth of Mahone Bay. An 8-kilometre passenger ferry service runs from Chester to Big Tancook and Little Tancook islands. The ferry offers an unparalleled way to experience the beauty of the bay, and once you are on either island there are many kilometres of quiet country roads and walking trails that offer ever-changing views of the bay and the gently rolling island landscapes.

Once a favoured hiding place for pirates Chester's neighbour, Mahone Bay is now noted for its colourful shops and boutiques, its restaurants and cafes and its well maintained century old homes.

These three photos of a classic, east coast motor yacht and its matching tender have formed a certrepiece of Chester Harbour for years and they perfectly reflect the spirit of this wonderful town.

MAHONE BAY

The unmistakable feature of Mahone Bay has to be the three churches lined up along the waterfront. Seen as you enter town from the east or west, St. James Anglican Church established in 1873, St John's Lutheran Church in 1866 and Trinity United Church in 1885, will leave you with an everlasting impression of Mahone Bay.

Mahone Bay is famous for its wooden boats and three wooden churches.
John McQuarrie

Just when you thought you had heard of all the possible themes for a festival, somebody comes up with another winner. Mahone Bay's Scarecrow Festival fits this category perfectly. These two examples are the proof.
John McQuarrie

Cape Breton's Margaree River Valley, (left) enveloped in an early morning mist, is a Mecca for fly fisherman from around the world.   John McQuarrie

Aerial view of Fortress Louisbourg National Historic Site. John McQuarrie

Dauphin Gate and interior view of Fortress Louisbourg. John McQuarrie

Step back in time to 1744! Experience Louisbourg, a thriving seaport and capital of Ile Royale, today known as Cape Breton Island. During the height of the French regime, the Fortress was the third busiest port on the continent and one of France's key economic and military centres in the New World.

The settlement had a population of about 3200, 700 of which were soldiers. Hugging the shore of the Atlantic Ocean, Louisbourg must have been a lively place, with its mix of Bretons, Normans, Basques, Germans, Swiss, Irish and the occasional Mi'Kmaq Indian visitor. For most, the big attraction was the abundant supply of cod that brought great wealth of the colony. But alas, nothing lasts forever.

France and Britain declared war in 1744; and the next year, attacking the fortress from the rear, the British captured the area after a six-week siege. In 1749, the French regained Louisbourg through a treaty and improved its fortification. But in 1758, again attacking from the rear, a massive British force of 30,000 reclaimed the fortress. In 1760, the British blew up the fort and in 1768 they withdrew from Louisbourg, as its strategic position was no longer significant.

The site was ignored for two centuries until 1961, when the federal government decided to reconstruct one-fifth of the original settlement. Today the site is alive and well once again. Since only 20% was rebuilt, you can clearly see the remains of the other parts of the fortress, despite being overgrown with time. In many ways, looking at what once was, is as interesting as experiencing the restoration. The site remains a massive archaeological time capsule which stands today as North America's largest historical reconstruction.

Talcum powder sand of Black Brook Beach north of Ingonish. Visitors to Ingonish should plan on driving to this spot with a thermos of coffee in the pre-dawn darkness to savour a sunrise that will more than justify leaving your cozy motel room in the dark. John McQuarrie

After visiting this part of Canada many times and interacting with the locals, I truly believe each and every person born in Cape Breton was blessed with the ability to either sing, play an instrument, (most likely the fiddle!) or dance! You can also insert any combination of the above for a lot of folks! To look around the island, at the highlands, the rivers, the coast, the beaches or the faces of the elders, is to look at the inspiration of these singers, songwriters, poets, musicians and dancers. They've been at it for hundreds of years, and there are still hundreds of years of inspiration left in the landscape. Deep down though I have to confess that the reason I really like this part of Cape Breton is because of Highland Links, one of the finest golf courses in Canada. This is a classic course, always ranked in the top five of the country, and right next door to the famous Keltic Lodge. The views, the wildlife, the moose, the deer and the ball stealing foxes, all combine to make this a paradise for the golfer.

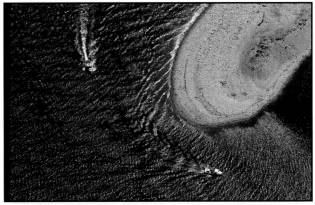

Aerial and ground views of Ingonish lobster boats. John McQuarrie

Cabot Trail winding its way south along the western shore of Cape Breton Highlands National Park, just a few kilometres north of the Acadian town of Cheticamp.   John McQuarrie

Cape Smokey on the Cabot Trail, just south of the lovely seaside village of Ingonish. John McQuarrie

You only *think* you're in the Scottish Highlands! Nova Scotia's Cabot Trail, in the Cape Breton Highlands is as breathtaking a drive as you'll ever make, and is considered one of North America's top scenic marine drives. The loop, which makes up the trail, takes you right through Cape Breton Highlands National Park. Here you can stop for a short hike to the rocky edge of the ocean or linger for a day hike on one of the park's many trails. There are country inns and bed and breakfasts everywhere and charming little villages like Ingonish, Margaree Harbour and Cheticamp. You could drive the entire trail in half a day, but don't! Take your time.   In fact, drive it in both directions The villages and towns won't change, but the view surely will.

Cap Rouge showing her stormy side. Sherman Hines / Masterfile

The trail was named for the famous explorer John Cabot who first spotted Cape Breton in June of 1497. As you drive take advantage of the many lookouts along the way. Otherwise you may miss a pod of whales, hundreds of shore birds including bald eagles and a seal or two – or two dozen – frolicking in the ocean. The route is diverse, offering an ever-changing panorama of lakes, forests, bogs and tundra along with the ever-present seascapes.

The natural beauty of Cape Breton provides a perfect setting for the mingling of Gaelic culture with Canada's diverse ethnicities and the result is an island of Old World charm. Its wealth of coastal vistas, wilderness trails, glorious beaches and pastoral vignettes make it one of the most intriguing vacation spots in North America.

In addition to all this spectacular beauty the towns and villages on the Trail each seem to have a festival or tradition they embrace every summer. It's just another part of the Cape Breton Highlands experience.

Six views of the Cabot Trail as you transition from the interior of the Park to the dramatic shoreline along the Gulf of St. Lawrence. John McQuarrie

BADDECK

Golden glow of sunrise illuminates Baddeck Bay on Bras d'Or Lake.   John McQuarrie

Alexander Graham Bell National Historic Site Visitor Centre overlooking Baddeck Bay.   From the grounds you can enjoy the spectacular view of the shoreline and waters of Bras d'Or Lake, where Bell made history and spent much of the last 37 years of his life.   John McQuarrie

The translation of Cape Breton's Bras d'Or Lake is "arm of gold" and this is one lake that clearly lives up to its name. Taking advantage of this magnificent setting is the picturesque resort village of Baddeck. First settled by loyalists in 1785, this town of 8,000 owes much of what it is today to a man who fell in love with the area in the late 1800's.

You may have heard of this guy. His name: Alexander Graham Bell. Bell first came to the Baddeck area in 1885, returning the next year to establish a vacation home for his family. *Beinn Bhreagh*, is a short hop across the bay, and stands to this day. Bell had already invented the telephone by the time he came to Cape Breton so money was not an issue. He branched out doing experiments in such areas as sound transmission, medicine, aeronautics and marine engineering.

In 1909 the efforts of Bell and three others culminated in the first powered flight in Canada. The plane was the *Silver Dart*. The village of Baddeck reaped the benefits of Bell's love for the area. Apart from putting the town on the map, Bell generated a significant impact on its economic and social life through his activities at *Beinn Bhreagh*.

During his life, Bell travelled the world. Here's a quote from Cape Breton's most famous resident. "I have traveled around the globe. I have seen the Canadian and American Rockies, the Andes, the Alps and the Highlands of Scotland, but for simple beauty, Cape Breton out-rivals them all". Bell and his wife Mabel are buried on the grounds of *Beinn Bhreagh* and the estate remains under private ownership to this day.

If you have an interest in kayaking – and this area is a great place for it – check out the folks at North River Kayak just outside Baddeck. They can take you out and show you the remains of one of Bell's wooden boats on the shore of St. Ann's Bay. There's not much left of it, but what a piece of history! Speaking of history: just a short drive from Baddeck you will find the Gaelic College of Arts and Culture, the only Gaelic College in North America. South Gut St. Ann's - population 64 - is the actual home of the college. Baddeck can also be used as a start/finish point for the famous Cabot Trail, one of the nation's most spectacular drives.

John McCurdy taking flight in the Silver Dart on February 23rd, 1909. This is the only surviving photo of the first powered flight of an aeroplane in Canada (and the British Empire). The gentle hillside visible rising from the shore of Baddeck Bay is now the site of the Alexander Graham Bell National Historic Site Visitor Centre pictured at left. National Archives of Canada PA61741

View to the west across St. Anns Harbour, Cape Breton. John McQuarrie

Aerial view of car ferry Bluenose approaching Yarmouth. The high-tech 'Cat' (below right) replaced Bluenose in the late 90's on the Bar Harbor, Maine run.

World's largest scallop fleet, Digby.

Fort Ann National Historic Site, Annapolis Royal. www.parkscanada.gc.ca

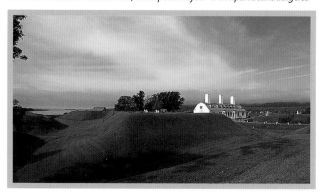

Fishing village, Yarmouth Harbour.

Historic buildings on Dock Street, Shelburne.

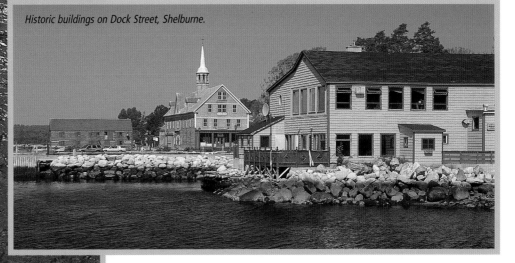

Dominated by the sea, the southwestern tip of Nova Scotia from Shelburne through to Yarmouth and around to Digby and Annapolis Royal, offers visitors an array of charming villages, lighthouses and dramatic coastal vistas. Along the way you will also encounter a number of national historic sites that explain Acadian and United Empire Loyalist influences on the history of Atlantic Canada. Your route here is another great drive. The Evangeline Trail follows Nova Scotia's Fundy Coast. If whale watching is in your plans, a side trip to Digby Neck is in order. You'll know it on the map when you see it! This drive also takes you through the Annapolis Valley, Nova Scotia's most fertile agricultural area complete with vineyards and apple orchards.

All photos: John McQuarrie

Yarmouth Lighthouse and museum at Cape Forchu.

The high-tech 'Cat' preparing to depart Yarmouth for Bar Harbor, Maine.

PICTOU

Marina and Hector Heritage Quay.   John McQuarrie

Located on Nova Scotia's Northumberland coast, Pictou is a town with a colourful history. It's known as the 'birthplace of New Scotland". In September of 1773 the first Scottish settlers, 33 families and 25 single men – 189 passengers in all – arrived aboard the *Hector*. This began a wave of immigration that would have a lasting impact on the cultural heritage of the province.

The story of this voyage, and it wasn't easy, can be discovered on the beautiful Pictou waterfront at the Hector Heritage Quay. The centrepiece is the full-scale three-masted sailing ship, a replica of the *Hector* which carried those first settlers on their voyage from Loch Broom Scotland so long ago.

Pictou, of course, has a *Hector* festival every August, during which they recreate the landing of the ship and feature Scottish music, dance, food and crafts.

You can also see that the village of Pictou is a blend of the old and the new. In this case the old clearly wins out! On the right of this picture you will note a trim, and modern Bank Of Nova Scotia. Beside it, a grand piece of architecture from the turn of the century that is the old Bank Of Nova Scotia. Sometimes older is just better!

Walker Inn and the old Bank Of Nova Scotia building. John McQuarrie

St. Margaret's Bay seems to have more than its share of lovely sunsets.
Sadly, a few weeks after the large photo was taken, a hurricane destroyed
this picturesque fish house at Indian Harbour. John McQuarrie

GRAND-PRÉ

In Canada's history the 1600s and 1700s were a time of almost constant conflict between English and French factions. In the mid 17th century a group of Europeans, mostly from France, settled in the area of Port Royal on the Bay of Fundy. The children born to these settlers came to be known as Acadians and today several million people can say they are proud descendants of this original group.

As the capital of the colony, Port Royal was often the scene of conflict. A small group of Acadians, weary of living under constant threat of attack, moved to Grand Pré, French for Great Meadow. Here they prospered. In 1713, a part of Acadie became Nova Scotia and fell under British control. The Acadians chose to live under British rule and were asked to take an oath of allegiance, an oath that became a bone of contention over the next 40 years. Things came to a head in 1744 when England and France once again declared war, and over the next decade, the British became increasingly concerned to have such a large French population surrounding them. In 1755, the British deported more than 6,000 Acadians from Nova Scotia. All property was confiscated and villages burned to the ground. This would continue for eight years until peace was made.

Church and statue of Evangeline, Grand Pré. John McQuarrie

EVANGELINE

Today Grand Pré stands as a national historic site to commemorate the Acadians of the Minas Basin and the events that forced them from their homes during *Le Grand Dérangement*, the "Great Uprooting". A statue of Evangeline stands in Grand Pré. She is the fictional heroine of the Henry Wadsworth Longfellow poem of the same name that told the story of a young Acadian girl from Grand Pré separated from her betrothed by the deportations. The poem, published in 1847, touched the hearts of countless people world wide and Grand Pré, which had been forgotten for almost one hundred years, soon became a popular destination for American tourists looking to visit the birthplace of Evangeline. Sadly, the only thing left of Grand Pré at that time was farmland and old willow trees. Finally, in 1963, the historic site became a reality. Today the gardens, the monuments, the church with its paintings, stained glass and the exhibits in the new visitor centre, tell the story of the Acadian people. It is a story of happiness and success, of sadness and tragedy.

In 2003 a royal proclamation, signed on the Queen's behalf by Governor General Adrienne Clarkson, offered regrets and healing words over the brutal treatment of the thousands of French-speaking Maritimers during the deportations. It recognizes the wrongs that were done and proclaims the 28th of July as the "Day of the Deportation".

NEW BRUNSWICK

SACKVILLE

One of the most unique city green spaces in all of Canada is located in Sackville. In describing the Sackville Waterfowl Park the town's web site says it best: "Discover a wetland world beneath your feet! Watch a muskrat part mirror-smooth water in a V-shaped ripple. Focus your camera on the antics of fuzzy ducklings dabbling in the shadows. Listen to a sunset chorus of marsh birds, the eerie cries of rail, coot, grebe and bittern. From dusk to dawn, the entertainment never stops...."

This park is unique in many ways, not the least of which is its location in the centre of town. That's no big deal but the busy Trans Canada highway forms the park's eastern boundary and is in plain view to all who drive by! But don't just drive by! This 55-acre park is home to 160 species of birds and over 200 plant species, and is easily traversed via its 3.5 kilometres of walking trails.

The highest tides in the world, twice a day, everyday, are seen in the Bay of Fundy, the body of water separating the provinces of New Brunswick and Nova Scotia. At their highest, with the gravitational pull of a full moon, the tides rise and fall some 14 to 16 metres at the eastern end of the Bay of Fundy, in the Minas Basin of Nova Scotia (photo above) and Chignecto Bay in New Brunswick. This phenomenon occurs because the Bay of Fundy is relatively shallow and narrow and the ebb and flow of the ocean tide pushes water in and out in a span of only 12 hours. Tides at the mouth are five metres and go up as you head into the ever-narrowing bay.

With water constantly moving and churning up the bottom, humpback, fin, minke and right whales have come here to feed every summer for thousands of years. Shorebirds and sea life flourish.

Moncton looking to the north over the muddy bottom of the Petitcodiac River.

Even though Moncton is more than 50 kilometres up the Peticodiac River from the Bay of Fundy, its famous tidal bore causes the river level to jump 7.5 metres in less than an hour as the tide waters surge over the mud flats.

Low tide in Minas Basin, Five Islands Provincial Park. Daryl Benson / Masterfile
Aerial view of Flowerpot Rocks at low tide and high-tide view from observation deck of the Hopewell Rocks Ocean Tidal Exploration Site. John McQuarrie

At the sandstone flowerpot formations at New Brunswick's Hopewell Rocks, you can walk on the ocean floor, then return later to see your footsteps washed away by the incoming high tide. It's a real experience to explore the seabed on foot in the morning, then sea kayak over the very same area in the afternoon, with the water now some 10 to 14 metres higher.

Seafloor at Hopewell Rocks Tidal Exploration Site. John McQuarrie

In the three images of the seafloor at Hopewell Rocks above, we see a father demonstrating to his children just how swiftly the tide rises in the Bay of Fundy. Within only a few minutes the little point of rock he is standing on momentarily becomes an island before vanishing beneath the surface.   The remaining photographs on these two pages show high and low tide comparisons in Alma and on Grand Manan Island.

116

High and low tide in Grand Harbour on Grand Manan Island. John McQuarrie

High and low tide in Alma Harbour.

GRAND MANAN

Located 35 kilometres off the coast of New Brunswick, Grand Manan Island stands guard at the entrance to the Bay of Fundy. The island is only accessible by a 90-minute ferry ride, which departs from Black's Harbour about an hour east of Saint John. Your Grand Manan adventure actually begins on this ride because on a clear day you might spot whales or porpoises right from the passenger deck! As you approach North Head get ready for a postcard perfect view of Swallowtail Lighthouse.

Most of the island's 3,000 residents live on its east side, an area alive with wild flowers and meadows. The west side is, for the most part, inaccessible and uninhabitable. Fishing, aquaculture and dulse gathering are the traditional industries here, but tourism is the growth business as more and more people discover the delights of the island.

Fishing boats pass Swallowtail Point at sunrise. John McQuarrie

Aerial view of Swallowtail Lighthouse, Black's Harbour. John McQuarrie

When we visited a whale watching tour that departed from North Head, it was the highlight of our trip. The high churning tides of the Bay of Fundy make for great whale watching because food is always being lifted from the bottom by the ebb and flow of the tide. Those same churning tides however, can be dangerous. The waters around the island have become the final resting place for over 300 ships over the past two centuries.

Classic dory used in the harvest of Dulse, a salty seaweed delicacy, silhou-etted by setting sun at Dark Harbour. John McQuarrie

CARAQUET

It's Acadian! It's authentic - and it's 400 years old!

All of New Brunswick was once part of Acadie after 1604, when the first French colony in the New World was established here. It was a harsh life - a story of triumph over tragedy. But through their difficult historical journey, the Acadians' "joie de vivre" sustained them, and their indomitable spirit is still celebrated in kitchen parties filled with fiddle music, traditional dance and storytelling.

The Festival Acadien de Caraquet, Caraquet's Tintamarre, the Blessing of the Fleet and the pilgrimage to Sainte-Anne-de-Bocage are all part of the Acadien celebrations here. Acadian spirit and pride is evident throughout Atlantic Canada, particularly in the imaginative ways the Acadian flag is displayed.

You'll see them everywhere Acadians live, the stella maris flag--the French tricolour with a single gold star in the field of blue.

Fishing fleet at Caraquet wharf with Chaleur Bay in the background. The five inset photos below reflect the wide diversity to be found in the fishing boats of Atlantic Canada– from the large, industrial trawlers to the smallest, one-man, wooden boat. John McQuarrie

SAINT JOHN

Saint John from the Fort Howe Lookout, site of an English fort built in 1778. *Greg Stott / Masterfile*

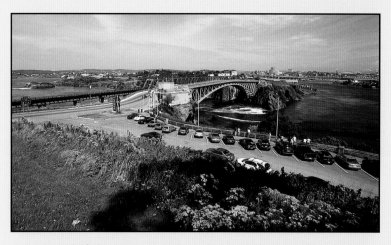

Restaurant and gift shop at Reversing Falls. In this view the incoming tide is causing the river to run upstream while, in the aerial view below, the flow is downstream during low tide. John McQuarrie

Discovered on St. Jean Baptiste day in 1604 by Samuel de Champlain and named accordingly, Saint John became the first incorporated city in Canada in 1785.

Home to one of the busiest and deepest ports in Atlantic Canada, its oil terminals serve some of the largest ships in the world. Tides in the harbour rise and fall some 5 metres so you could be sitting in one of the cozy waterfront restaurants watching as ships disappear or reappear with the tides. Waterfront redevelopment has brought this part of the city back to life as old warehouses have been transformed into shops, boutiques and restaurants.

The famous Reversing Falls might be a bit of a misnomer but it is impressive and certainly worth a look. The spectacular water show is created where the Saint John River flows into the Bay of Fundy. At low tide, the river falls some 16 metres into the bay. Then, as the tide rises, there is a period of slack when the water in the river and the water in the bay reach an equal level. But that lasts less than half an hour before high tide begins to push the mighty Saint John River into reverse. The tide rises another 4 metres creating swiftly moving rapids that now flow upstream. Hence the name.

Saint John is also a city of great walks. Self-guided tours take you downtown in the footsteps of the city's Loyalist founders and through turn of the century commercial and residential areas. Like much of Atlantic Canada, the city gets more than its fair share of fog in the summer, but you just can't beat an evening stroll in light rain and mist as you meander through the city's history.

Carleton Martello Tower National Historic Site offers a spectacular view of Saint John. John McQuarrie

Both the Fort Howe Lookout and Carleton Martello Tower offer great views of the city along with a glimpse into the past. The Tower is a national historic site; its familiar, circular profile visible from most parts of the city. Completed in 1815, it served in defence of Saint John Habour until 1944.

No visit to Saint John is complete until you've wandered through the historic City Market. This is the oldest continuing farmers market in Canada, serving the community since 1876. When you walk into the building, look up! The signature feature of the market is its roof, an architectural wonder. The system of rafters were built from hand-hewn timbers and assembled in the same manner as a ship's hull, albeit upside down. And don't forget to try the dulce when you're there. Many New Brunswickers consider this dried out seaweed a delicacy. I had a little different reaction, but you be the judge!

Restaurants lining the west side of Loyalist Plaza. John McQuarrie
Interior view of the Saint John City Market. John McQuarrie

Morning light near Jemsing. Freeman Patterson / Masterfile

There is something – call it a feeling – about the Maritimes that is hard to put into words. There's a feel and texture to the place that you just don't encounter anywhere else. When you visit, you sense it. The warmth of the people, the warmth of the light of day, the warmth of a sunset, and knowing how to savour what nature provides. It's a place you can take the time to walk through natural and human history. A place where you can be a million miles from home yet feel like you are home. A place to listen to dancing fiddles, thumping feet, strumming guitars and rich voices that echo out for no reason other than it feels good.

To make a living from the sea, but not take away from the sea. To protect what they have, yet at the same time share their land. To hear songs written from the heart about the pride of living in Atlantic Canada, where people play the cards they are dealt as if every hand were four of a kind. Canada's smallest province is here, and so are some of Canada's smallest cities. More people live in Winnipeg, Manitoba than in all of New Brunswick. The city of Kitchener, Ontario has more people than Prince Edward Island; and the population of Halifax proper, the largest city in Atlantic Canada, is just under 120 thousand. No one here thinks that's too small, and no one would want it any other way.

Morning light, Kingston. Freeman Patterson / Masterfile

A rising sun silhouettes the boardwalk of 'La dune de Bouctouche' at the Irving Eco-Centre just north of the town of Bouctouche. John McQuarrie

One of the many unique attractions that dot the east coast of New Brunswick is the Irving Eco-Centre : La dune de Bouctouche. The white sand dune that stretches 12 kilometres across Bouctouche Bay is a result of the constant action of wind, tides and sea currents since the last ice age. After every major storm its shape changes. This environmentally significant area is the habitat for a rich variety of marine and aquatic plants and animals, and for shorebirds and migratory birds.

Created to celebrate the fictional characters of renowned novelist and playwright Antonine Maillet, Le Pays de la Sagouine (left) is an island of legends, music, and theatre celebrating the rich Acadian history in the Bouctouche area.

La Pays de la Sangouine, Bouctouche. John McQuarrie
Entrance to the two kilometre long boardwalk of the Irving Eco-Centre.

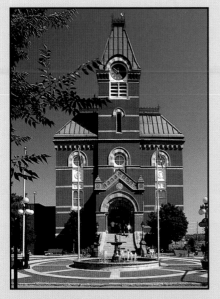
Fredericton's City Hall. John McQuarrie

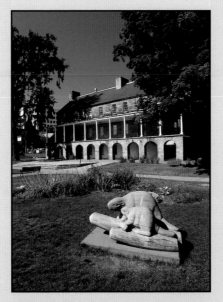
Officers' Quarters, Fredericton. John McQuarrie

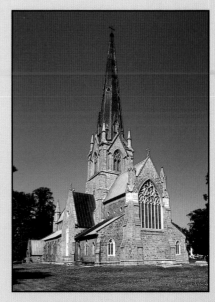
Christ Church Cathedral. John McQuarrie

*Charming outdoor cafe, St. Andrews By-The-Sea.
John McQuarrie*

Fredericton is the capital of New Brunswick. Located on a bend on the scenic Saint John River, it's one of the oldest settlements in North America. It was first inhabited by Maliseet Indians thousands of years ago. Like St. Andrews-By-the-Sea, United Empire Loyalists also settled here in 1783 and it's been the provincial capital since 1785. The Old Government House and Historic Garrison District have been named both provincial and national historic sites. The city is renowned for its architecture, culture and heritage.

Canada's oldest seaside resort town is the delightful St. Andrews By-the-Sea, tucked into the southeast corner of the province. The signature landmark is the Fairmont Algonquin Hotel. Built in 1889, it overlooks not only the village but also picturesque Passamaquoddy Bay. And it may or may not be true that room 473 of this hotel is haunted, but certainly search out one of the town's ghost story tellers and find out if it's true!

The Algonquin, a renowned Canadian Pacific Hotel now part of the Fairmont chain, is St. Andrews' dominant landmark. John McQuarrie

St. Andrews By-The-Sea

Like many seaside communities throughout the region, the government dock at St. Andrews By-the-Sea is the focal point of both recreational and commercial boating activity. The extreme length of this pier is mandated by the legendary Fundy tides that expose the sea floor here right out to the end of that dock.

St. John's Chapel. John McQuarrie

The delightful St. Andrews By-the-Sea is one of the loveliest in the Maritimes and a treasure trove of beautiful architecture. It was founded in 1783 by United Empire Loyalists who chose to remain loyal to the British Crown following the American Revolution. Many crossed the bay to their new country with all their worldly possessions, including – for some, – their homes, which they dismantled and rebuilt here. Some are still standing today. Over 250 buildings in St. Andrews' downtown are between 100 and 200 years old. The entire town was designated a National Historic Site in 1998.

Water Street, St. Andrews. John McQuarrie

The dam and old red mill of St. George. Shortly after the dam was built, a salmon ladder was installed to benefit stocks of wild salmon that migrate up the Magaguadavic River to spawn. The ladder has enabled a serious conservation effort to protect and enhance the wild salmon run.
John McQuarrie

Just west of the provincial capital of Fredericton you'll find King's Landing. Located in the Saint John River valley, it's a place to step back in time in a recreation of an historical settlement spanning the years from 1820 to 1890. Here you will find more than 70 buildings, including a gristmill, old English pub, historic homes, print shop, school, church and a wheelwright's shop. More than 100 costumed guides are there to help you make your way through the village and its 70 thousand artifacts. You could ask the wheelwright to make a new wheel for your wagon! In 1968, an 80-kilometre section of the Saint John River valley was flooded with the opening of the Mactaquec Dam. Most of the buildings at King's Landing were rescued from this area and preserved to give a living, breathing glimpse of life in New Brunswick in the 19th century.

Aerial view of King's Landing. John McQuarrie

Bill Brooks / Masterfile

John McQuarrie

J. A. Kraulis / Masterfile

At 391 metres, or 1,282 feet, the longest covered bridge in the world spans the Saint John River at Hartland New Brunswick. Built in 1901, the bridge was originally uncovered for some 20 years. After ice destroyed two spans in 1920, the bridge was covered two years later to increase the life of the span. Many refer to covered bridges as 'kissing' bridges, and certainly all 900 people who live in Hartland could easily be accommodated in this one for a smooch or two! Some historians suggest the term originated because the covered bridge offered couples an ideal spot for privacy and darkness at night, before returning to the residential streets of the city. One can only imagine how many horses ran out of gas in the middle of the great Hartland Bridge!

Bridges weren't covered for romantic or aesthetic reasons; but rather, for practical ones. Uncovered bridges of the era began to fall apart after 10 years due to the elements – sun, ice, snow, and rain. Covered bridges, on the other hand, were expected to last for at least 80 years or longer, as the Hartland Bridge has proven. Another reason to cover a bridge was to calm horses which could easily be spooked by the rushing water below. The covered bridge offered the comforting atmosphere of a barn.

World's longest covered Bridge crosses the Saint John River at Hartland.
John McQuarrie

Kingston Creek. Freeman Patterson / Masterfile

CAPE ENRAGE

Is there a better name for a place in all of Canada than Cape Enrage? Perched overlooking the Bay of Fundy, halfway between Hopewell Rocks and Fundy National Park, Cape Enrage is home to the oldest lighthouse on mainland New Brunswick. It has been in continuous operation since 1848. I arrived at Cape Enrage one warm, sunny day in June. One half hour later, the fog was as thick as pea soup and the wind was strong enough to bowl you over! But this is the beauty of the Cape, a place to witness the awesome forces of nature that rule the Bay of Fundy (and I also got to hear – close up unfortunately – the famous Cape Enrage foghorn!).

After the lighthouse was automated, the out-buildings here fell into a state of disrepair and it looked like they were destined for demolition. Fortunately, in 1993 a group of students from Harrison Trimble High School in Moncton adopted the complex and began an ambitious restoration project. It took two years, but in 1995 it was up and running again, as good as new. Their goal remains preservation and protection of the heritage lighthouse. Today, they continue their involvement by operating a non-profit organization, which runs a restaurant on-site and offers rock-climbing and kayaking adventures.

Cape Enrage also offers one of the great rappelling adventures in New Brunswick. I wasn't nervous as I stood, backwards, on the edge of the rock cliff, with a 130-foot drop straight down to the rocks below. At least I don't think I was! When you're strapped in and ready to go, it's best to go! And go I did, three times that day. You can go rappelling no matter what the weather, but only at low tide. If you go when the tide is high your finishing point would be under five metres of water!

Built in 1838, Cape Enrage lighthouse is the oldest in mainland New Brunswick. John McQuarrie

GRAND FALLS GORGE

Pontoon tour boat exploring Grand Falls Gorge, Grand Falls. Photo courtesy of Department of Tourism and Parks,

Visitors to Grand Falls Gorge are always amazed by the spectre of these dramatic cliffs towering 70 metres above the Saint John River in this otherwise pastoral part of New Brunswick.

The gently rolling potato-farmland surrounding the gorge, together with the calm and meandering river, offer no clue to the existence of such a dramatic canyon.

PRINCE EDWARD ISLAND

Fishing boat departing Naufrage Harbour.

Naufrage harbour.

Aerial and beach level views of the Confederation Bridge. John McQuarrie

CONFEDERATION BRIDGE

Taking a ferry to get on – or off – Prince Edward Island was a way of life for hundreds of years. But that all changed in 1997, when the Confederation Bridge linking PEI to New Brunswick officially opened. Crossing the Northumberland Strait is now a 10 minute drive over the 12.9 kilometre span, as opposed to long line-ups for an hourly ferry that was weather-dependent and always busy. The highest point on the bridge is 60 metres above the water while the average is 40 metres; but despite extreme high winds that regularly plague the strait, its robust construction means the bridge has only rarely been forced to close.

The bridge has a hollow core that acts as a utility corridor for electrical, telephone and other services to the Island. PEI, with no train tracks since 1989, now has goods transported to the island in minutes. The real winner has been tourism. People are flocking to PEI in record numbers to enjoy the world famous seafood, beaches and historic sites. They can also bike and play a few rounds on the island's ever-expanding array of golf courses. When travelling over the bridge, be sure to look for the bridge construction grave yard on the right as you enter PEI. Many concrete remnants and bridge forms are lined up in eerie fashion, a la Stonehenge – an isolated ode to a remarkable engineering challenge and achievement.

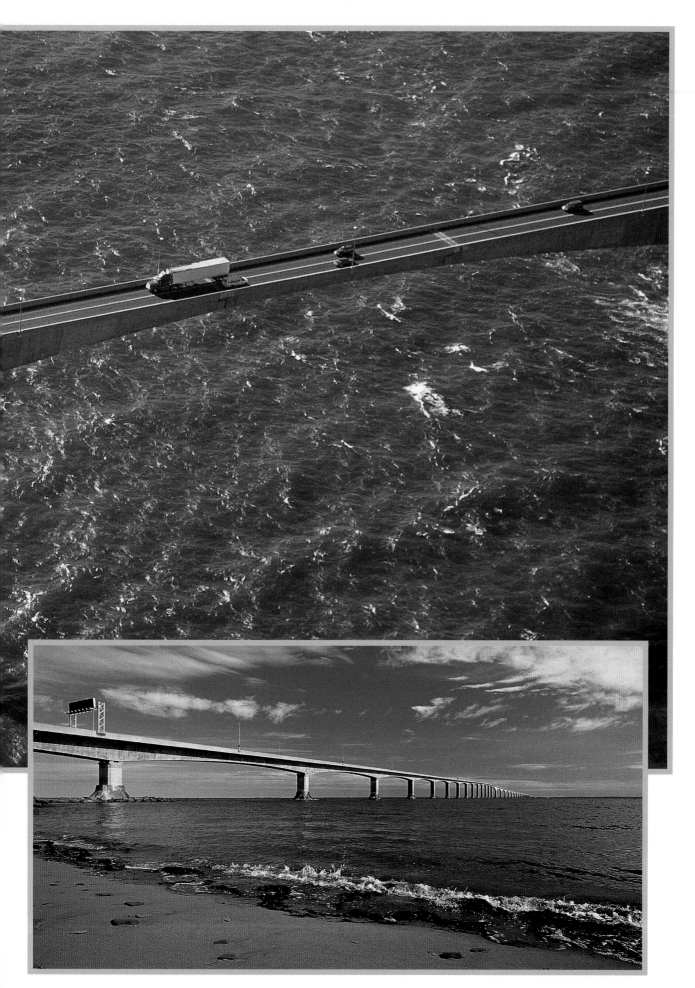

CHARLOTTETOWN

Built to commemorate the birth of Canada, Confederation Landing is a collection of marinas, restaurants and parkland.
John McQuarrie

Peakes Wharf, Charlottetown waterfront.
John McQuarrie

Historic Charlottetown, the "Birthplace of Confederation", is Canada's smallest provincial capital with a population of just under 40,000. But don't let its size fool you. This is one vibrant city, blending the old with the new; and one that underwent a renaissance when the waterfront was redeveloped. The centrepiece is now Confederation Landing, a collection of marinas, restaurants, shops, boutiques and parkland. Founder's Hall is close by and it is in this fine exhibit that one can get an entertaining and informative perspective of the birth of a nation. In addition to Province House National Historic Site, Charlottetown boasts the Confederation Centre of the Arts. It is here that the legendary story of Anne of Green Gables is presented along with other fine stage works throughout the year.

Charlottetown also gets much of its charm from places like Victoria Row, just behind the Arts Centre. This old warehouse district has been completely restored and buzzes with outdoor patios and quaint shops. Summertime is magic here and don't be surprised if your meal on the open patio is accompanied with music by a jazz ensemble.

In 1864, the Fathers of Confederation met at Province House in Charlottetown to discuss the politics and economics of founding a nation. It is a fascinating story.

Cafes and shops of Victoria Row.   John McQuarrie

Province House National Historic Site of Canada was built to house the Prince Edward Island legislature, a function it has served continuously since its official opening in 1847. In 1864, the Fathers of Confederation met in this building to discuss the union of the colonies that would ultimately lead to the formation of Canada on July 1st, 1867. Ironically, the meeting was originally scheduled to discuss the union of the three Maritime provinces – New Brunswick, Nova Scotia and Prince Edward Island. When the Maritime colonies agreed that their own union should be the subject of the conference, Canada – then consisting of an uneasy union of Ontario and Québec – seized the opportunity and her governor wrote to ask if the Canadians might attend.

The Union Proclamation, 1873. Courtesy Dusan Kadlec ©

The Maritimes set the date, September 1, 1864; the Canadians were invited to make their presentation, and the rest is history. There is considerable evidence that the hospitality offered to the delegates by the citizens of Charlottetown had a powerful influence on the eventual outcome. The spirit of goodwill engendered by powerful politicians meeting each other on a matter of such attractive common interest was enhanced by the sincere and lavish hospitality that met them at every turn. Lunches on the Canadian steamer, *Queen Victoria*, home entertaining by their Island hosts culminating in a banquet by the City of Charlottetown, kept the delegates in a euphoric mood. They enthusiastically journeyed on to Halifax and agreed to meet again in Québec.

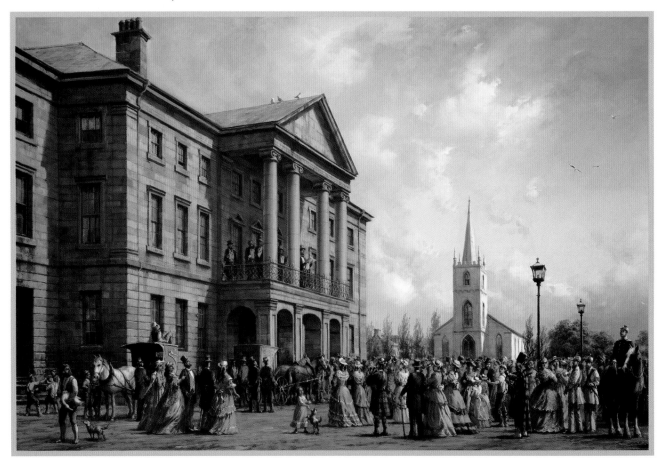

Historic homes comprising the 'Inns on Great George', a collection of 11 buildings offering unique accommodations to visitors. John McQuarrie

Prince Edward Island (PEI) joined Confederation on July 1, 1873. Despite their long resistance to union, many Islanders celebrated the day. Buildings throughout Charlottetown were decorated with flags, bunting and streamers. At noon there was a brief ceremony at the Colonial building, where the union proclamation was read, and the crowd sang the national anthem. Islanders, however, still retained a strong sense of independence. When Lord Dufferin visited Charlottetown later that month, he was so impressed by the Islanders' lingering sense of independence that, he reported he was "under the impression that it is the Dominion that has been annexed to Prince Edward Island."

Everything here is within walking distance and you can start your tour with a stroll up Great George Street to historic Province House. In doing this you will be following in the footsteps of the Fathers of Confederation who, upon arriving at the docks, walked this same route to their meeting with destiny. On your way, notice the wonderful old buildings on either side of the street. Many of them were in place on that momentous day back in 1864.

While in Charlottetown many of the Fathers of Confederation ate and slept in small inns along Great George Street in the city's downtown core. Visitors today can follow in their footsteps by checking into the Inns on Great George. Rather than a single inn, the Inns on Great George is actually a collection of 11 historic buildings, each with its own story to tell. The Wellington House (Circa 1811) was a downtown pub during the Confederation Conference. Another building, the Pavilion was an operating hotel where many of the Fathers of Confederation slept.

The larger of the two photos at left offers a view down Great George Street from inside the lobby of Province House. Charlottetown Harbour can be seen sparkling in the distance and, apart from the cars, the view would have been much the same during those history-making days in 1864. Now look closely at the slight dip visible on the floor of the entrance. The smaller photo is a close-up detail of a depression in the soft sandstone. It was created by the soles of the millions of pairs of shoes and the hobnailed boots of farmers that have passed through this historic entrance for over 150 years.

On the final night of the conference, September 8, 1864, the City of Charlottetown hosted a banquet and ball in Province House which had been transformed for the occasion from political arena to grand hotel. The legislative council chamber, where the delegates had so recently reached their landmark agreement, now served as a gracious drawing room.

Refreshments were available in the library while the assembly chamber was transformed into a ballroom with evergreens, flowers and flags. There, under the brilliant gas light, delegates and their partners danced to the music of two Charlottetown bands playing in the gallery above.

Province House Ball, 1864. Courtesy Dusan Kadlec ©

At midnight the throng adjourned to the ground floor supreme court-room where a magnificent banquet was waiting. Toasts and speeches expressed the goodwill and optimism felt by the delegates after their week of discussion.

Farmhouse at Green Gables. John McQuarrie

ANNE OF GREEN GABLES

Let's play a word association game. When I say Prince Edward Island, you say? Well, if you're like millions across Canada and around the world, your answer is Anne of Green Gables. PEI author Lucy Maud Montgomery wrote *Anne of Green Gables* and twenty two other books starring the orphaned red haired, pigtailed heroine Anne. The books were about Anne's life and times in and around the fictional PEI village of Avonlea. While Avonlea exists only on the page and in the hearts and minds of readers worldwide, Lucy Maud Montgomery based Avonlea on the small north shore town she grew up in; picturesque Cavendish.

Today, visitors from around the world flock to Cavendish for the Avonlea experience and to visit the homestead which has been restored to portray the Victorian period setting in which Mongomery grew up. In 1943, Montgomery was recognized by Canada as being a person of national historicial significance. Just outside Cavendish, in New London, the birth place of Lucy Maud Montgomery is open to the public. It's still in great condition, and stands ordinarily at the junction of two roads, in a village with just a few other houses.

Just outside the village you'll find jaw-dropping seascapes featuring PEI's famous red sandstone cliffs and the entrance to Prince Edward Island National Park which, like Cavendish, is located on the Gulf of St. Lawrence, part of the Atlantic Ocean. A favourite of hikers and bikers, the park features, beaches, stunning red cliffs, sweeping wind blown sand dunes, salt marshes and woodlands.

Birthplace of Lucy Maude Montgomery, author of 'Anne of Green Gables.
John McQuarrie

Aerial view of farmhouse at Green Gables. John McQuarrie
Anne's bedroom in the farmhouse. John McQuarrie

"Cavendish is, to a large extent, Avonlea. Green Gables was drawn from the David MacNeil's house, though not so much the house itself as the situation and scenery, and the truth of my description of it is attested by the fact that everyone has recognized it"
L.M. Montgomery, *The Selected Journals of L.M. Montgomery*, Vol. II, Friday January 27, 1911.

Cavendish Beach, Prince Edward Island National Park. John McQuarrie

Even with an influx of tourists, a deserted beach is easier to find than a crowded one on PEI. Since you're never more than 20 minutes from the water, getting to the shore is no problem! From the world famous beach at Cavendish, to the signature dunes at Basin Head, to the sheer expanse of Prince Edward Island National Park, there's a beach to suit all those looking to pack their worries away for an hour, a day or a season. Sands of white, pink, red and champagne greet you at the seashore as yet another lonely lighthouse evokes thoughts of mariners past. Family outings seem to come alive when the kids' bare feet first hit the talcum powder smooth sand.

Here they can run and laugh to their heart's delight with no worries that a tumble in the soft sand will be a problem – just a burst of more spirited laughter. And no matter how loud their shrieks of delight, the wind will carry them away with only the occasional seagull complaining. And all this exercise, combined with great gulps of fresh, salt laced air will guarantee the kids a sound sleep, allowing the parents to sneak out in the pre-dawn darkness the next morning for a sunrise stroll amidst gently rolling waves lapping up on shore. Same beach but with an entirely different feeling at this magical hour!

Beach and dunes at the O'Sullivan estate, Lakeside. John McQuarrie

Talcum powder beach typical of Prince Edward Island National Park. John McQuarrie

Dunes and characteristic red sand of Prince Edward Island National Park. John McQuarrie

Covehead Lighthouse, Prince Edward Island National Park. John McQuarrie

Cavendish Beach offers visitors a tantalizing wealth of wetlands, sand dunes and of course, endless stretches of talcum powder sand. It is not surprising that everyone who comes here on a lovely summer day such as this is quick to remove shoes and socks in response to the irresistible invitation of the place.

Aerial view of Cape Tryon Llighthouse. John McQuarrie

North Head Lighthouse. John McQuarrie

Panmure Island Lighthouse. John McQuarrie

West Head Lighthouse. John McQuarrie

Panmure Island Lighthouse. John McQuarrie

I found Victoria By-the-Sea quite by accident while driving in PEI. We were looking for a 'back way' from Charlottetown to the Confederation Bridge and traveller's luck led us to this quaint little village with a population of 158. What a find! It's a four block setting of charming homes and businesses complete with art gallery, pottery studio, chocolate factory, candle shop and craft stores.

Victoria Wharf and shops. John McQuarrie

The picturesque wharf with several shops and a restaurant is also home to the town's fishing fleet.   If this isn't enough the Victoria Playhouse, housed in the historic community hall, presents several plays throughout the summer.

If someone showed you these photos and asked you what part of Canada they were from chances are your answer wouldn't be "Prince Edward Island".

On my first visit to PEI, I certainly had a pre-conceived notion of what I would find here. Flat, red soiled farmland, lots of potatoes, a couple of beaches and a bunch of stuff about a girl named "Anne". I should throw lobster in there as well, because a co-worker of mine returned home to Summerside for two weeks every summer and he never failed to talk about lobster, all the while extolling the virtues of the island. I wish I had listened sooner and more closely. There's a reason "Islanders" always come back home.

Much of the province is a stunning blend of rolling hills, farms with fields strung out like a patchwork quilt, quiet rivers and wetlands complemented by ocean bays, sand dunes, flora and fauna and seascapes that end off in the distant horizon. It's an island of solitude; an island that sees first hand the power of nature; an island of gathering; and most of all, an island of friends.

And hey! There's a ski hill on Prince Edward Island! Come off the bridgehead to Charlottetown and hang a right at Crapaud. It's on the right, halfway to Cavendish. In fact, just a bit further down the road you'll come to Hunter River where one of these pictures was taken. By the time you get across the island to Cavendish, you'll wonder why it took you so long to get here.

Morning mist on Hunter River in town of Hunter River. John McQuarrie

Morning mist on Hunter River near New Glasgow. John McQuarrie

Sunrise in fog silhouettes house and barn near Brookfield. John McQuarrie

Morning fog lingers over Hunter river near New Glasgow. John McQuarrie

Potato fields near Seaview. Gary Black / Masterfile

The signature landscape of Prince Edward Island is its gently rolling fields and iron rich red soil, a combination allowing PEI to harvest some of the best potatoes in the world. Farming, fishing and tourism are the island's three main industries and as you can see by this spread, PEI is also a photographer's delight.

The island is 224 kilometres long and anywhere from 6 to 64 kilometres wide. Water is never far away. Red soil is everywhere. It's not hard to get lost in the beauty of it all. Charm oozes from every nook and cranny of the island, dotted with picturesque farms, church steeples and quaint shops. At water's edge you can find some of the world's best mussels and oysters and, in places like New Glasgow, North Rustico, and St. Ann's, busloads of tourists come for world famous lobster suppers.

Rich red soil furrowed and ready for planting potato crop, Springbrook.
Dale Wilson / Masterfile

Potato crop several weeks into the growing season, Springbrook.
Gary Black / Masterfile

Barn and tractor near Glenwood. Daryl Benson / Masterfile

From Tignish in the west, to Elmira in the east, the Confederation Trail is a haven for bikers and hikers throughout the summer. Once bustling with noisy train traffic the trail, with tracks removed, is a serene adventure taking you truly off the beaten path – throughout the length and breadth of the island – to see places once reserved for brakemen and engineers.

French River harbour and farmland near Brookfield. John McQuarrie

Rusticoville harbour.
John McQuarrie

Fishing fleet, North Rustico. John McQuarrie

New London harbour. John McQuarrie

One of the aspects of travel that remains with us longer than most is a particularly memorable view, one that you know at the time will go into that special drawer in the backroom of your mind. The stillness and surreal beauty of this twilight vista of North Rustico Harbour made my lobster supper, taken on the far end of the pier pictured at right, all the more enjoyable. And the shoreline of Prince Edward Island National Park can be counted upon to dish up sunsets, as in the inset photo at left, with remarkable regularity.

John McQuarrie

Heading for Home, 1921. Courtesy Dusan Kadlec ©

For the countless millions of people who have enjoyed exploring the area around Peggy's Cove on a perfect, summer afternoon, we decided to leave you with a wintery view most people will never experience. It also gives us a chance to indulge ourselves and sneak in yet another image of one of our favourite places in Atlantic Canada.   And for all of you who survived the record big snow of 2004, this image - and the one on page 67 - were taken a few days after the storm. Jeff & John

Also from Magic Light Publishing:

Best Of Canada
By: Jeff Hutcheson
$15.95 (ISBN: 1894673115)
Soft Cover, 8" by 11", 160 pages,
over 200 colour photographs
Photographic portrait of Canada
from coast to coast.

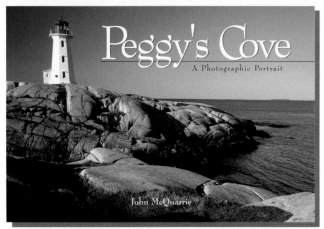

Peggy's Cove
By: John McQuarrie
$6.95 (ISBN: 189467314X)
Soft cover souvenir booklet, 32 pages

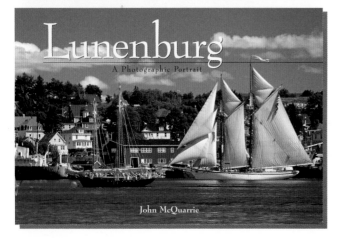

Lunenburg
By: John McQuarrie
$6.95 (ISBN: 1894673158)
Soft cover souvenir booklet, 32 pages